You've Been Fired! Now What?

Seize the opportunity, creatively turn it into a Successful reality

"Transform a job seeking challenge into wealth-creation opportunities, with 33 principles & proven systems for business success."

By

Tonia Askins and Victor Kwegyir

International Business Consultants

Published by 21CECGC Publishing
14241 Coursey Blvd, Suite A-12 #249, Baton Rouge, LA 70817
www.21cecgc.com

ISBN: 0988389002
ISBN-13: 978-0-9883890-0-7
ISBN-13: 978-0-9883890-1-4 (ebook)

Printed in the United States of America & United Kingdom
Library of Congress Control Number
2 0 1 2 9 5 3 7 6 8

To request Victor and Tonia for speaking engagements,
interviews and consultations please send an email to
vito@21cecgc.com

21CECGC books are available at special discounts when
purchased in bulk for promotions as well as for educational or
fund raising activities.

Dedication

I dedicate this book to my husband Daryl for his continued support, patience and devotion to me for this great project. Knowing that service is my passion, you have allowed me to do all that is in my heart, and I am grateful. To my children, Anaya, John and Aiden, thanks for giving mommy the time to write, I Love You. To my dear Mother, Margaret who has also supported me throughout my life, teaching and allowing me to believe there are no limits, Thank You. To my wonderful mother-in-law, Diane, I will be forever grateful for the wonderful example you are as a tremendous human being, Thank you can never be enough for what you have brought to my life. My business partner for this great project cannot go without being thanked. Victor, from the first time I heard your interview, I knew the extraordinary gifts that were inside you. Thank You for everything. Last but certainly not least and above all I thank God and my Lord and Saviour Jesus Christ for giving me the insights, compassion and orchestrated opportunity to birth the gift of writing and in doing so help others identify theirs. — *Tonia*

I dedicate this book to all my family and clients, who constantly inspire me to learn and strive for heights and excellence in what I do; to Pastor Matthew Ashimolowo, my spiritual father, who by his thumb of approval on what I do gave me a huge platform and opportunity that I do not have enough capacity to measure its worth; and lastly to God and Jesus Christ my LORD and personal saviour without whom the ability to write will never have been awakened. — *Victor*

Acknowledgments

Writing this book has been such a rewarding experience and I must give credit to those who have paved the way and help define who I am today.

Thanks to my family and friends for all the love and support throughout this project. My sisters and brothers (Earnest, Jeanine, Trunean, Robert & my late brother Thomas), and the Cade family.

To Herman and Beverly Mitchell for your continued prayers and spiritual guidance.

To the Jesse Duplantis Ministries family for the great opportunities, teachings and tremendous blessings.

Bernell Charles Jr. of Charles Investments LLC for the very first assignment and support of all my endeavours.

To all my clients, you all have been tremendous in allowing me the honor to serve and represent you whole-heartedly.

To all fellow and aspiring entrepreneurs for your continued motivation and inspiration.

To all the wonderful leaders and business owners that I have worked for that shared, taught, mentored and believed in me from such a young age. Thank you, I hope that you are proud. — **_Tonia_**

I will also like to thank all those who directly or indirectly influenced my thinking in embarking on this project with my co-author.

Thank you Tonia for following up after the radio show and connecting with me for us to work together. You were like an angel sent at the exact moment I needed inspiration and support, albeit a perfect professional partner to work with. You are such a creative and intelligent person to work with.

Thank you Pastor Ade D'Almeida for everything you have been to me. Your counsel, support, challenge, thoughts and shared ideas have been exceptionally helpful.

Thank you Michael Ajose for the encouragement, support and the invaluable friend you are.

Thank you to all friends and loved ones who have been supportive over the years, especially my wife - Coretta, Mum - Agnes Kwegyir, Mother in-law – Maame Christiana Fokuo, Sisters (Theodora, Natalia, Dorothy, Marian and your wonderful families), Rev & Mrs Peter Bacha, Mr & Mrs Kwame Banful, Mr & Mrs Kennedy

Dosomah, Mr & Mrs Paul Nifah and Mr & Mrs Kemba Agard. I am very grateful to you all. — *Victor*

Finally to all those that have been stressed and displaced during these challenging economic times, we have heard you loud and clear. Be encouraged, this one's for you.

Introduction

Business and life globally has changed dramatically over the last couple of years, and who knew that many people would be in a position that would forced them to quickly adjust without having much time to digest the situation.

We believe that there has never been a better time to explore a world of opportunities in business that most would never have dreamed of. The enormous possibilities of today's technological advances have given us unlimited access and a vast platform that connects people, places, and concepts worldwide. By embracing these developments, we expand our capacity to reach and take our rightful place in today's business economy.

In this book, we provide an overview of what it means to be in business and stay in business. We shed light on the process, provide examples of successful entrepreneurs, showcase situational case study examples, and share a wealth of informative business advice and support. Whether you allow your abilities, talents, and experiences to undergird you as you test the entrepreneurial waters or dive in headfirst is your choice.

This book provides the challenge, tools and insights to assist you along the way.

Most people have pondered going into business for themselves at one time or another, but most stop after that point without researching whether the concept they are considering is viable or profitable. Recall the many times you pondered starting your own business or creating opportunities for others by way of your dreams but never followed through. Our challenge to you is to follow through with those ideas and abilities and develop innovative ways to create your own future.

The book also explores the benefits of starting your business at this time in the global economy. It helps you dissolve apprehensions that may stop you from decisions that can positively affect you, your family, and others around you. Your options depend largely on your knowledge base, skill set, passion, and goals; these will get you from milestone to milestone even if you consider any of them insignificant. The key is momentum. Challenges are inevitable, but the way you handle them and react (or not react) to them will determine how they impact what you are seeking to achieve. You will find that in going into business for yourself, the biggest challenge is *you*. This has been one of the main driving forces in striving to help others by way of this collaborative entrepreneurial focussed project.

The experience gained from challenges and the clients we have been privileged to assist over the years has helped us to get out of *"our own way"*. The beauty of this project for us, as international consultants, is the knowledge that the growth process in business is a constant, and assisting others along the way is a joy.

Take the opportunity *now* to create your future and tap into the possibilities that are around you.

Contents

Chapter 1

What Happened?

It is not unusual to find uncommon weather patterns across the globe these days. Summers can be exceptionally hot or have record level rainfalls and winters can be very mild or exceptionally cold with unprecedented heavy snow. On comparison, as we write from two continents, the heightened levels of unpredictability seem to be the same.

Interestingly it has been almost the same sense of unpredictability for most economies, as news feeds stream daily across the globe. Although we both live in different nations – UK and US, we are constantly privy to stories and witness the distress of those who have been impacted by the instability of national and global economies.

One day, it's the Euro zone crisis. Another day, it's how the Chinese economy growth rate has been slashed. Not to forget weekly and monthly US job data figures either rising a bit higher or falling below expectations. These lift the mood in the market or shake the confidence of market players.

To most of us, it sounds as if there is an individual whose mood swings are all that matters; he must be treated with care, otherwise any slight twist in the news makes him happy or unhappy. Often times it looks like the stream of economic data from around the world have a hard time ensuring this person's "happiness."

Today, the impact of uncertainty in one national economy on the other is more pronounced and swift due to advances in technology. A piece of news in one corner of the globe can cause a major market swing elsewhere in seconds.

In Appendix I and II are news stories and statistical economic data that reflects the nature of the dramatic changes in the economies and unemployment conditions around the globe.

International Labor Organization defines unemployment as "people aged 16 and over who are out of work, want a job, have actively sought work in the last four weeks and are available to start work in the next two weeks; or are out of work, have found a job and are waiting to start it in the next two weeks."

Interestingly anyone who falls under the above definition is part of a family, and these families are part of society, some of whom we may know, that is, if we do not happen to fall in this percentage category ourselves.

As former employees we are familiar with this state, having been laid off at one time or the other, we had to "face the music" of being classified as unemployed. Unless an employable individual has made up his mind not to work, unemployment is very much a concern. According to former UK Prime Minister, *"unemployment is of vital importance, particularly to the unemployed."*

The question of why some are unemployed or what led to layoffs may not cross your mind and the impact not felt until you or someone close to you are handed a 'pink slip' (US), or 'P45' (UK) or 'C4' (Belgium) - (a discharge notice in an employee's pay envelope to notify the worker of his or her termination of employment or layoff). The reasons for the layoff vary from organizational downsizing to businesses on the verge of bankruptcy.

In an attempt to explain the problem of unemployment, Craig Bruce, a business coach, said, *"Why are people unemployed? Because there is no work. Why is there no work? Because people are not buying products and services. Why are people not buying products and services? Because they have no money. Why do people have no money? Because they are unemployed."* Calvin Coolidge, the thirtieth US president, *said, "When a great many people are unable to find work, unemployment results."*

Our focus in this book is to help you who may find yourself in a similar state. We both have experienced unemployment at some point in our professional lives, and our desire is to assist others make quality decisions during a critical economic period regardless of education, industry, or experience.

Whether you have completed high school or earned a doctorate, are a stay-at-home mom or dad, or professional woman or man on the go, neither unemployment nor entrepreneurship discriminates.

Our desire is to offer hope and give you tools so that the economic system does not frustrate your dreams or inhibit your ambitions.

The best way to safeguard against unemployment is to make informed choices and create the future you desire. This book offers a wealth of guidance whether you are thinking of becoming a business owner by choice or because of circumstances beyond your control. If you haven't solidified your decision due to inhibitions, this book will help you see how you can realistically begin the process.

Let's take a look at some of the issues people are grappling with in the midst of the unstable economy.

Alicia, twenty-two years old, bookstore attendant
Alicia has worked part time at the local bookstore for two years. When sales hit an all-time low, she was one of the first employees to be let go. She was work-

ing toward her associate's degree, and her aim was to work part time to help pay her school expenses while raising her three-year-old son. How would she cope after being laid off? Is this familiar?

Jeffery, forty-six years old, automobile factory executive

Jeffery was in management in the auto industry for close to fifteen years when he was let go due to downsizing and low sales. He's been married for twenty-two years to his wife, a schoolteacher, and the father of five. His wife's income is only enough to pay half of the family bills. What could Jeffery and his family do?

Rhonda, eighteen years old, salesperson at an electronics store

Rhonda is a single parent, striving for a better life, with only a high school education. Her work hours were reduced due to a decrease in sales. How could Rhonda take care of her children on a reduced salary? What choices would she have in addressing this challenge?

Veronica, twenty-seven years old, airline industry midlevel manager

Veronica worked her way up the corporate ladder and was comfortable after landing a role in management. Due to the economic downturn, she was given two options: step down and receive lower wages to keep her job, or take a severance package of half a years' salary. She was shocked and wondered, "How did it come to this?" How could she address this situation?

Samuel, fifty-nine years old, securities industry senior market analyst

Samuel worked half his life in securities. He was shocked when replaced by a twenty-nine-year-old recruit who would work for half of Samuel's salary. Samuel felt lost and despondent, completely unsure of what to do, especially given his age.

Cleaners INC, 5 years, cleaning business

Cleaners INC., providing contract-cleaning services to local companies. Their major contract was with an electronic retail giant that has gone bankrupt. A loss of this size contract may cause the company to go bankrupt and the owner is at a lost for what to do.

Kenneth, thirty-five years old, restaurateur

With a major slowdown in sales, Kenneth had to lay off a few servers and considered taking a part-time job to keep the business of his dreams open. Due to the financial outlook of the industry, he believes that business would and could pick up soon. In this position, what can Kenneth do to help his company get on track?

William, twenty-nine years old, designer clothing distribution manager

William was laid off because of the decrease in demand for high-end ladies apparel and accessories. He had worked in the industry for eight years and was the breadwinner for his family. At the end of the month, the bills were due. Wondering what he's done wrong and how unfair life seems, he's asking himself, "Now what?"

Rocky, twenty-four years old, IT developer

The youngest in his office, Rocky had an enterprising social media mind set. Because of the firm's six-month financial projections, his hours were reduced. He had planned to save money for personal projects including a new developer software, but the decreased hours brought just enough income to pay his living expenses. How can Rocky increase his earnings?

Yashira, twenty-five years old, graduate student

Yashira completed her master's degree in education and received a job offer from the local school board for an entry-level administrator position. Yashira dreams of opening a day care and is torn between starting her own business or taking the position. She and her fiancée of two years plan to start a family in five years and knows that time is of the essence. Her offer letter states that she has to accept or deny the offer in thirty days, "Now what?"

Thomas, forty-five years old, insurance agent

Thomas was a military veteran. After completing his tour of duty, he received training in the field of insurance. He was primary caretaker of an adopted niece and his elderly father. Thomas pondered purchasing the brokerage firm he works for, because the owner plans to retire, but he is leery. Unsure of what to do, Thomas began researching other options and discovered that the initial investment to start from scratch is $15,000. With $10,000 in savings and $86,000 in his 401k account, his dilemma is whether to go forward or not.

We can identify with these stories. You may also relate with them personally or know a friend or family member who has been caught up in similar circumstances.

Accept the fact that unemployment is not permanent unless you choose to make it so. We will take you through an eye-opening journey, share practical steps and vital processes, and describe how we as well as others creatively took hold of the opportunity.

It is not over, you can creatively turn this around.

Chapter 2

Now What?

"Most of the important things in the world have been accomplished by people who have kept on trying when there seemed to be no hope at all."–**Dale Carnegie**

———

Most people are shocked by a layoff, reduction in hours, or other unexpected job shift. Usually it takes time to get through the actuality of the event and into a productive mental prospective to move forward. The transition can be challenging, but it is not one that you can't pull yourself through. The anger, disappointment, hurt, and resentment are all normal, and the process is different for everyone. After the shock wears off and the reality that the unthinkable has occurred, your transition begins. You can go forward, standstill, or back track mentally about the occurrence.

Usually at this stage, focused planning may also be hampered by emotional and physical factors. For most people, the stress levels increase, mental and emotional changes show up and as a result the following feelings may be experienced:

- Loss of self-worth
- Loss of daily purposeful activity
- Loss of professional identity
- Loss of work-based social network
- Loss of financial security

At some point you will contemplate the "now what?" question.

- Do you give up?
- Do you search for other employment opportunities?
- Do you take the opportunity to further your education?
- Do you sit home and collect unemployment benefits/job seekers allowance?
- Do you examine viable business possibilities?

Let's briefly assess your options.

Do you give up?

Yes, you could give up, if you have nothing to live for, have no aspirations, or have no financial and/or family obligations. We have yet to come across anyone who has no obligations, so giving up cannot be an option. Our primary focus here is to help you make the best out of the situation and gather fresh momentum for growth and success.

Do you search for other employment opportunities?

Seeking new employment is the most common first choice option for the unemployed and anyone who is not satisfied with their current state of employment. However, when there are mass layoffs across all sectors, where do you look for a new job? In January 2011, Federal Reserve Chairman Ben Bernanke said, *"It will take four to five years to get back to normal unemployment."* A year later, in his testimony to Congress, Mr. Ben Bernanke reiterated, *"Notwithstanding the better recent data, the job market remains far from normal."* This admission among others (*refer to* Appendix II) coupled with more weekly announcements of layoffs, suggests that finding a new job may be challenging for years to come.

Do you take the opportunity to further your education?

This option is great, but it has its challenges, due to the significant dependency on steady income in most households. According to a BBC report, in a Downing Street media conference at the height of the economic crisis, the former UK Prime Minister, Gordon Brown, addressed the subject of long-term employment: *"We are being tough in saying it is a duty on the unemployed in future not only to be available for work, and not to shirk work but also to get the skills for work. That is a new duty we are introducing."*

If you choose education or obtaining new skills, you will probably do so while looking for ways to earn some income during the process. Your choices remain to find employment or entertain creative ways to earn income.

Do you sit home and collect unemployment benefit/job seekers allowance?

You can, at least until you choose your next productive step for earning income. Contacting your area job centre or benefits office as soon as possible after job loss is recommended, due to the processing time. We understand how challenging this can be and the embarrassment it can make you feel, even though the predicament is not your fault. Although this "stop gap" measure may be available in developed economies, the same cannot be said of every economy. These benefits are temporary and have maximum terms of compensation and qualifying requirements.

Do you examine viable business possibilities?

The possibility of self-employment or starting your own business as a sustainable option is the focus of this book. For most people, knowing where and how to start can be daunting if not approached from the right perspective. Records and well-researched facts show why we believe this is among the best options. In subsequent chapters, we will discuss extensively the benefits of going into business and the very advantages the current economic downturn presents to anyone who dares to take that leap of faith.

In Appendix III are some supporting facts that emphasize why the time is ripe for starting a business.

In addition to the advantages the economic downturn presents, available technology also provides a wealth of information, opportunity, and assistance from seasoned entrepreneurs who are willing to share experience-based advice and help you on the journey.

There are tremendous benefits in equipping yourself with great resources and thought-provoking tools. Opting for self-employment or starting your own business is not just about jumping on the next "get rich quick" scheme. It's about locating viable opportunities that exist, leveraging the skills you possess, and others you may want to develop, so that you can offer the best quality products and services to those who need them.

As you contemplate, remember to keep in mind the basic market principle of supply and demand. For instance, if you have skills in industries that are on the positive end of the market spectrum, you have a great opportunity to develop a business with those skills in mind. The possibilities also exist for you to take current news and industry projections to creatively extract business ideas.

You can get through this stage by empowering and building yourself up through resources such as this book. We challenge you to rise up and create your own destiny.

> *During pivotal moments, the key is not only making a decision to move forward but also making the right decisions during the move.*

There is light at the end of the seemingly endless dark tunnel—you have to press forward to see it. Oscar Wilde once said, *"what seems to us as bitter trials are often blessings in disguise."*

Chapter 3

The Way Forward

"Tomorrow belongs to the people who prepare for it today."–**African Proverb**

———

Most people who experience a loss or transition in employment have mental and emotional issues to overcome as well as the issue of exploring new opportunities for income. Shock, hurt, anger, and disappointment are all common feelings after an employment shift, but rest assured that there are ways to move past them. Moving forward in a constructive way is important for clarity and mental stability. Your decisions will require focus and planning and, for the best results, a consistently positive outlook.

Maintaining an optimistic mind set of success will be an advantage in moving forward and being proactive.

Your journey will be filled with planning and properly applying the information you've gathered. Allow yourself to go through the emotional process, knowing that you will get through it. Here are some steps to aid you:

1. Accept the situation.
2. Decide to move forward.
3. Be positive.
4. Take inventory of yourself.
5. Set a daily schedule.
6. Participate in activities that support who you are at your core.
7. Keep your speech and mind set in the present and future, moving through any adverse feelings about the past. Focus on good times, life lessons, and work experience. Building your future starts with your thought process today.
8. Be consistent!

"When it comes to the future, there are three kinds of people: those who let it happen, those who make it happen, and those who wondered what happened," says Professor John M. Richardson, Jr.

If you continue to feel overwhelmed or unable to get a grasp on your emotions, it's not uncommon to seek professional guidance. Counselling services are available at workforce centers/job centers throughout the US, UK and most developed economies at no cost to qualified individuals. Many also provide additional services such as:

- Career counseling
- Computer and Internet access

- Certification programs
- Program information for veterans
- Training and skills opportunities
- Information on salary trends

The benefits of going forward with a focused mind set are tremendously beneficial. Allow yourself to go through the process as patiently as possible but with consistency and steadfastness, one day at a time. Abraham Lincoln said, "*The best thing about the future is that it comes only one day at a time.*"

Developing a successful thought process by building your confidence as you decide what to do next will be rewarding. Harness the power within, knowing that there is a world full of opportunities. How life will turn out for you is created first in your mind, followed by the actions you take toward making it happen.

The desire to succeed is not a guarantee to becoming successful.

Choices, not circumstances, determine whether or not you succeed.

Congratulations on your progress for coming this far. You must be already contemplating the road of entre-preneurship. Let's explore the options so that you can grasp the potential pathways and possibilities.

Chapter 4

Benefits of Starting a Business

"Nothing is more pleasing and engaging than the sense of having conferred benefits.–**Ellis Peters**

—⋙—

Opting to start a business is an experience many have embraced. Although it can be demanding, especially in the early stages of establishing yourself, it could become an interesting learning curve. A lot will depend on how you can turn the journey into a memorable experience. Alberta Flanders once said, *"Sometimes only a change of viewpoint is needed to convert a tiresome duty into an interesting opportunity."*

Irrespective of what you think of the process, if you have a business idea worth pursuing, starting a business is a worthwhile option. Like any pursuit in life, people are most encouraged and challenged when they are clear about what they stand to gain from realizing a dream. Let's highlight some of the benefits that await you on this remarkable journey.

Benefits of Starting a Business

Understanding the benefits of entrepreneurship should encourage you in acting out your dream. Although a few specific benefits may differ slightly from community to community or nation to nation, some of the most compelling benefits are as follows.

1. **You are your own boss.** You get to be in control. The demands of having to stick to certain routines and procedures are no more. You can direct your business the way you want it, in line with your dreams and passions. You control and influence every aspect such as, the best hiring process, the personality and skills of the employees you are comfortable working with, working hours, management style, and the other factors that determine how the business operates.

2. **You have personal time.** You get to manage your time to suit your personal life. You can plan around your child's daily school runs, your favorite community activities, hobbies, holidays, and other activities that are dear to your heart.

3. **You have flexibility.** Flexibility allows you to change course or adapt quickly to new opportunities without anyone else's approval. There is therefore no need to feed ideas up any chain of command.

4. **You have unlimited income potential.** You have no limit on the amount of income you earn, and you can pace the growth of your income according to your capacity to produce. The possibility of making more money progressively through your own business, rather than by working for someone else, is more obtainable.

5. **You can set your goals.** There is no limit to how successful you want to become. Your ambitions are limited only by your own desires. You can remain in a small business capacity or expand beyond your immediate environs.

6. **You can impact society.** You can create wealth and use it as you wish to influence society. In the words of Cullen Hightower, "*A true measure of your worth includes all the benefits others have gained from your success.*" Running your own business is your best bet in achieving this.

7. **You have reduced personal liability.** You have a reduction in liability, especially when setting up a Limited Liability Company (LLC) or corporation. Your personal assets are protected against possible company liability.

8. **You can pass on a legacy.** Businesses, in many instances, are deemed separate entities from their owners and directors and have a perpetual existence. They can therefore be passed on to

your children whereas you cannot do this with a job.

9. **You control your destiny.** By having your own business, you have a sense of ownership and hold your destiny in your own hands. This provides a keen sense of purpose.

10. **You have reduced tax liability.** Some expenses you would have paid from a salary can be allocated as business expenses.

11. **You can have lifetime income.** Your company can generate perpetual income even after retirement.

12. **You are a lifetime employer.** Owning a business gives you an opportunity to be an employer for life, thus positively influencing the lives of others. As an employer, you help your community and nation deal with unemployment while potentially providing employment for individuals and families.

13. **You can support your cause of choice.** Through your company, you can give to the cause of your choice (charities, educational institutions, etc.). For those who are passionate about charitable causes, no joy compares to setting up your own business and generating the income to fund your vision or support others in theirs.

14. **You have job security.** You are relieved of the thought of ever being *"fired."* The challenge is to ensure that your business runs profitably and smoothly.

15. **You feel personal achievement.** The joy derived from creating and running a successful business can be exhilarating. As your business grows, the satisfaction of knowing that you did it from the ground up is far more fulfilling than building someone else's business.

16. **You are a problem solver.** As a business owner, your products or services provide solutions for your clients and society at large. As a solution provider, you earn respect in your community and nation.

All said and done, you owe it to yourself to take advantage of the immense benefits you stand to gain in starting your own business. It provides the opportunity to launch out and

With the right idea, knowledge, determination, and passion; you will succeed irrespective of your circumstances.

Chapter 5

Starting a Business in an Economic Downturn

"Conditions are never just right. People who delay action until all factors are favorable are the kind who do nothing."– **William Feather**

———

An economic downturn offers benefits to anyone wanting to start and grow a successful business, anywhere in the world.

Most world economies are unstable. In April 2012, The Wall Street Journals' "The Big Interview" show, host David Wessel asked the managing director of the IMF, Christine Lagarde, how she would describe the state of the world economy in one word. She said, "Unstable." She also said, "The IMF is raising its forecasts for global growth from levels it expected in January, but there is still a high degree of instability in the world economy." She highlighted the level of interconnectivity in the economies of the world, which makes it increasingly difficult for any single economy or nation that is seemingly doing well to be unaffected by the challenges of other economies. By October 2012, even China, which seemed to not have been touched by the recent crisis, saw its annual GDP growth fall to 7.5 percent from 9.3 percent in 2011, according to The World Bank Data report.

History has taught us that in such crises, fresh innovative ideas are born as a solution to the challenging times. Most of the billion-dollar businesses in existence today were established during the Great Depression, and the recessionary years from the 1950s to the 1990s.

In Victor's first book, *The Business You Can Start*, it highlighted statistics that emphasized how many major corporations took advantage of economic downturns to start and grew into successful businesses. Walt Disney Company, Hewlett-Packard Corporation, Microsoft Corporation, Proctor & Gamble, Burger King, General Electric, and Cable News Network (CNN) are notable examples.

"Challenging economic times can serve as a motivational boost to individuals who have been laid off to become their own employers and future job creators," said Carl Schramm, president and CEO at Kauffman. Bishop T. D. Jakes, the senior pastor of The Potter's House (a global humanitarian organization with a thirty-thousand-member church) and an entrepreneur, said, *"The greatest business opportunities are born in the middle of crisis."*

Historical records show that more people start businesses during recessionary times than any other period. Many such businesses survive, and some become corporate giants. Of course, there are times when conditions seemingly present themselves as more favourable for a new start up.

At the same time, the strength of your conviction and passion can help you ride the storms to safety, should you be determined and willing to make the needed adjustments on the way. Napoleon Hill once said, *"The majority of men meet with failure because of their lack of persistence in creating new plans to take the place of those which fail."*

These facts support the argument that economic downturn is not necessarily a barrier to starting a business. A downturn rather brings opportune conditions that, when exploited, can be a great platform for the start and growth of a business.

Let us explore some of the advantages that others are taking to start and grow successful businesses in such uncertain times.

1. **Solution provider.** Every business provides a solution to one of three problems: the problems of yesterday, of today, or of tomorrow. The current world economies, with great levels of uncertainty and problems, present huge opportunities for people to become problem solvers, thus creating business.

2. **Opportunity to test systems.** A downturn is an opportunity for a new business to "find its feet" and test its operational systems. By the time the

economy picks up and sales start to increase, the systems will have been adjusted, and the business can efficiently cope with customer requirements. If your business can thrive in a recession, imagine how it will soar when good times come again.

3. **Favourable competition.** Your potential competitors could be weakened and as a result, may close down or sell the business. If a hole develops in the marketplace, you may find an opportunity to slip into it, thus taking advantage of the reduced competition. However, you will need to do extensive market research to evaluate whether your product will survive, because the economy will eventually recover.

4. **Low cost asset acquisition.** Prices often drop during a downturn, making it the right time for fantastic deals on office furniture, office supplies, land and equipment.

5. **Reduction in cost of highly trained staff.** You can hire more and better-qualified people. When the giants are laying off, you can find great personnel at affordable rates. Is it your desire to form a professional service firm or hire a qualified accountant? Laid-off professionals such as lawyers, accountants, nurses, doctors, engineers, IT professionals, bankers, and investment advisors may be looking for new firms to work for, and most of them will potentially take a job at a reduced pay rate.

6. **Auctions and deals.** You can buy much of what you need at auction. Repossessions mean that large equipment, office furnishings and space, restaurant equipment, or other expensive items are offered at rock-bottom prices. For instance, you could get great deals on fleets of vehicles and trucks for deliveries, haulage, or construction.

7. **"New kid on the block" advantage.** There is an advantage in being the "new kid on the block" when it comes to pitching your product or service. Many companies are desperate to find partnerships with new companies with different, better, or more innovative ways of delivering products and services. Even if your prices are higher, you can present your products or services as having greater value.

8. **Opportunity to attract investment.** Most people (including your family and friends) may be wary of investing in stock or real estate markets. They may be willing to finance a portion of your new venture or the expansion of an enterprise that has proven itself over time. The main benefit is that they know you and have a relationship with you. Having a solid and competitive business plan that delivers real numbers means a better chance of attracting capital.

9. **Win-win supplier opportunities.** Most suppliers give better credit as they seek new opportunities. When credit markets are shaky or virtually shut down, the

business-to-business (B2B) credit flows keep money circulating out of sheer necessity. All parties have more incentive to find true win-win situations, ones that allow for cash and stock flow. When everyone is looking to survive, great deals can be executed.

10. **Most businesses are looking to change suppliers.** Suppliers of existing businesses might have gone out of business, thereby creating opportunities. The surviving businesses that depended on them need new sources for supplies to ensure smooth operations. By providing much-needed supplies at economically viable rates, you fill the gap.

11. **Media exposure.** Going against the grain in such times can provide prime opportunities for publicity. The media loves aberration, and if you are expanding or getting into business, you will fit that category. You can generate great PR by demonstrating your "alternative" view of the market. For instance, on a BBC Radio 5 Live show, host Anna Foster interviewed Lucie Balchin, who the "British Independent Retailers Association claims could be the youngest person to own a shop, the Crazy Cow gift shop in Modbury, Devon, England." The challenging times forced the original shop to close. Balchin grabbed the opportunity to start something on her own. This got the attention of the local media and the British Independent Retailers Association. The rest is, as they say, history.

12. **Negotiating power.** You can find great "low money or "no money down" deals. By being aware of good opportunities that others have overlooked, you could purchase a business by taking over a lease (along with all the equipment). Many business owners want out at any cost. You can negotiate win-win deals that allow the owners an escape, and you have the opportunity to turn around what could be, if run right, a viable business.

13. **Increased government support.** With unstable economies, many national, state, provincial, and municipal governments have embraced entrepreneurial development. They have promoted business-friendly policies including the Small Business Administration Act in the United States, the UK business growth accelerator program, and the introduction of the business bank by the UK Government Business Secretary Vince Cable. These policies and incentives are aimed at encouraging small business owners and potential owners to take advantage of the incentives and packages to start and grow a business.

All over the world, from the US to South Africa, governments are frantically establishing measures such as offering soft loans, grants, free training, business coaching programs, and tax breaks to small and upcoming businesses. In some cases, stringent regulatory requirements

are relaxed for the sake of encouragingjob creation. Fortunately, during these times there is a
lot of support to ease the hurdles when it comes
to starting a business.

14. **Market testing.** A downturn is a great time for a
new business to test whether its product or service is economically viable, and it proves what the
business can handle during challenging times.
This improves your chances of succeeding regardless of market conditions.

15. **Lower start-up cost.** The above advantages results
in having lower start-up costs during a downturn.
Your ability to negotiate win-win deals with suppliers, take advantage of auctions, negotiate deals on
leases for office space, and find discounts ensures
reduction in the cost of initial investment.

16. **Lifetime opportunity.** In an economic crisis, you
may have lost your job and been forced to seek
other income opportunities. Sometimes, the best
business decision is the one you are forced into,
and the incentive is often enough to push people
"on the fence" to strike out on their own. In the
words of Joseph Campbell, an American writer
and lecturer, *"Opportunities to find deeper powers
within ourselves come when life seems most challenging."* There's nothing wrong with being in this

position; it means greater urgency to do something that generates income as quickly as possible.

"You are surrounded by simple, obvious solutions that can dramatically increase your income, power, influence and success. The problem is, you just don't see them."— Jay Abraham

Open your eyes. Decide to look at things differently, start where you are, and make smart and informed moves toward the business opportunities around you.

With the right steps, you will take hold of your dreams and turn them into reality.

"Don't wait until everything is just right. It will never be perfect. There will always be challenges, obstacles and less than perfect conditions. So what? Get started now. With each step you take, you will grow stronger and stronger, more and more self-confident and more and more successful," says author Mark Victor Hansen.

Keep reading as we assist you in considering the options necessary to help you make one good choice after the other in starting the business of your dreams while increasing your earning power and scope of influence.

Chapter 6

Principles for Business Success

"An army of principles can penetrate where an army of soldiers cannot."–**Thomas Paine**

Businesses are started every day. Some have the rare privilege of "hitting the ground running" and creating sales almost immediately. Others take a while to sell their product or service. Some grow and become successful, others merely exist, and a sizable proportion, if not the largest, fail at their objectives.

Among those that fail, some go back to the drawing table and resurrect the vision, taking into consideration the experience gained. Others allow the failure to cripple the business idea and demoralize them.

Those who have the courage to start over want to

> *Learn from the experience of failure and adopt tried-and-tested principles from those who have succeeded.*

Most will confess that if they had taken more time and sought the advice of professional business advisors and successful business owners, they could have avoided some of the costly mistakes.

What we seek to share with you in this chapter are some basic principles and nuggets from our combined thirty-five years in business as owners and professionals, as well as that of other successful business people.

In the words of Jawaharlal Nehru, the first Prime Minister of independent India, *"Failure comes only when we forget our ideals and objectives and principles."* Your success depends on allowing the principles to guide you and form the core of your operational policies. Here are some valuable principles to consider.

General Principles

1. **Every business is a solution provider.** Every business provides a solution to the problems of yesterday, of today, or of tomorrow. See yourself as a solution provider, and add a lot of inspiration to what you do. Thomas Edison once said, *"I never perfected an invention that I did not think about in terms of the service it might give others...I find out what the world needs, then I proceed to invent."*

2. **Make no provision to quit.** Resolve to make no provision to quit. Be determined to endure the sacrifices required to establish yourself, become profitable, and succeed. In the words

of Jack Canfield, *"If you're passionate about what it is you do, then you're going to be looking for everything you can to get better at it."*

3. **Be a visionary.** It is important to establish your ultimate goal. *"People with goals succeed because they know where they're going,"* said Earl Nightingale. A clear vision will spur you on in the face of challenges. Your goal may be to become wealthy, retire comfortably, become a respected member of your community, or become an established brand that lives up to your values. A clear understanding of where you are going becomes a reference point that you always return to for inspiration and revaluation.

4. **Be passionate about your product.** Be passionate about your product or service. You are more likely able to convince others to believe in your product when you believe in it yourself. *"To be successful, you have to have your heart in your business, and your business in your heart,"* said Thomas Watson Sr. Your business will take a large part of your life, so you do not want to be doing something you do not enjoy. Clients notice whether or not you have a passion for what you are trying to sell them. Steve Jobs did put it this way: *"The only way to do great work is to love what you do. If you haven't found it yet, keep looking. Don't settle."*

5. **Successful business is built on integrity.** Business without integrity is like "building on sand." It is almost impossible to go far in business without integrity. A business might be legal, but find it difficult to justify the claims associated with its product or service. Customers see through you more than you think. Alan K. Simpson said, *"If you have integrity, nothing else matters. If you don't have integrity, nothing else matters."*

6. **Have a specific purpose for the business.** As a business owner, your business must have a clear, unique, and well-understood purpose. In business circles, purpose is seen as the fundamental proposition upon which the organization rests. This means that when employees know the purpose of the organization, they know how their jobs contribute to its success, and they are more likely to work together to achieve those goals. When an organization has its fundamental principles right, customers, clients, suppliers, regulators, and visitors feel that "these people know what they are doing."

7. **Appreciate your limitations.** It is equally important to know your own limitations. Establish what you can do well, and focus on it. In building the business, seek specialists for the areas that you do not do well. It may cost you more to fix a "half-baked job" than to hire a professional to do it from the onset. When starting out, you

may have financial constraints, but think outside the box. You may be able to negotiate a deal to obtain the service or product you need, pay for it later, or offer a product or service in return.

8. **Manage expectations.** It is important to manage your expectations from the onset. This enables you to be patient as you grow the business and avoid becoming frustrated at the smallest hurdle.

9. **Grow with the business, and work smart.** To grow your business, you must grow with it. Work smart, not just hard. Get as much information as you can to understand your business, the market, the processes, the customer needs, and the best practices. You have a greater chance of succeeding in business when you increase your knowledge of what you have to offer. Information is the key to business efficiency. Thomas Kalaris, CEO of Barclays Wealth and Investment Management, said, *"Fundamentally, the only competitive advantage one has is client knowledge."*

10. **Learn from your mistakes.** Instead of fretting and beating yourself up for mistakes you make, learn from them. Take the time to consider what you could have done for a different result the next time around.

11. **Establish a reputation of excellence.** Another important principle worth taking note of is, to establish a reputation of excellence. Excel-

lence at what you do and how you offer it is necessary for longevity in business. Harriet Braiker said, "*Striving for excellence motivates you,*" and Oliver Cromwell said, "*He who stops being better stops being good.*"

Marketing

12. **Make consumers want what you have to offer.** Identify those who need your product, and make them want it enough to spend cash on your business. To realistically take your share of the existing market, find a way to make consumers want what you are offering more than what others offer. Establishing your unique selling point is very important.

13. **Everything you do is marketing.** Marketing is not everything, but everything you do is marketing. Make sure that you have a clear business focus and a narrow, specific target market. Know exactly what you are selling and whom you are selling to. The answer to who you are selling to is never, "anyone who wants to buy."

Sales

14. **Highlight the benefits of your product.** Differentiate between the benefits and the features of your product, emphasizing the benefits and value in your sales pitch. Also, take notice of your features and highlight their benefits to the customer.

Pricing

15. **Customers pay based on the value they attach to the product.** A customer needs to see enough value in what you are offering to warrant paying the price. When customers say they do not like your price, it is not always because the price is too high. Rather, they don't see that what you offer warrants the price. When you help them see the value in what you offer, you boost your odds of success dramatically. In the words of Warren Buffett, *"Price is what you pay. Value is what you get."*

16. **Set the price from the onset.** When customers get used to a price point, it is more challenging to convince them to pay more. Rather than relying on pricing to make your product competitive, focus on adding value to your product. Also, in a contract situation, it is very important to work out your profit before you agree to the price on any contract.

Branding

17. **Have a branding strategy from the start.** Your visual identity and brand are the first things that your customers see. Your branding strategy should weave through your business from the start. It does not always cost money to be a good brand, but it does cost a lot of money to fix a failing or non-delivering brand.

18. **Let your brand distinguish you.** Build your brand by getting your prospects to see you as the only one who provides the solution to their problem rather than just choosing you over the competition. Brand strategist Kerry Light said, *"The primary focus of your brand message must be on how special you are, not how cheap you are. The goal must be to sell the distinctive quality of the brand."*

Competition

19. **Business is competitive.** Settle in your mind and heart that business is competitive. You will compete with other businesses, directly and indirectly, for the same clients. You are also competing with the customers' other expenses.

20. **Establish uniqueness.** Keep an eye on your competitors, but never do what they do. Position your offering as different from theirs.

Customer Care

21. **Focus on the needs of customers, not what you like to sell.** Seek every opportunity to bring smiles to your customers' faces. You will build a huge reservoir of goodwill and positive word of mouth at very little expense. Concentrate your efforts on the needs of the customer, not on what you like to sell. Caring about your customers gives you a high return on the time,

effort, and money you invest. In the words of Orison Swett Marden, an American writer and successful hotel owner in the late 1800's, *"The golden rule for every business man is this: Put yourself in your customer's place."*

22. **Invest in lasting customer experience.** To reap the highest returns and ensure a lasting investment in your brand, think of customer care as an investment, not an overhead expense. A lasting customer experience is a jewel in your arsenal. In the words of Jeff Bezos, founder of Amazon.com, *"If you do build a great experience, customers tell each other about that. Word of mouth is very powerful."*

23. **Allow customer care staff authority to resolve issues.** Never put customer care staff in charge of dealing with issues without adequate authority to make decisions and take the steps to rectify a situation. Anything short of that risks worsening the customer experience.

Business Systems

24. **Build a system.** Develop the right systems to run and operate your business. That way your business can function with or without your involvement.

Hiring Employees

25. **Hire people smarter than you are.** Hire with the ultimate goal and future of the

business in mind, and hire people who are smarter than you are. People are a company's greatest asset. *"It doesn't make any difference whether the product is cars or cosmetics. A company is only as good as the people it keeps,"* said Mary Kay Ash, the founder of Mary Kay Cosmetics.

26. **Hire people you can fire.** Hire with your gut and head in agreement, and hire people you can fire when they are not up to the task or committed to the company vision.

27. **Hire people with creativity in mind.** When you hire good employees, they will seek opportunities to be creative. For example, good employees know that when the line at the front desk is four or five deep, they must move the line expeditiously, but if there is no crowd, that is the time to add a little flare and conversation.

Funding

28. **Have a backup.** For smooth day-to-day business operations, consider contingency funding. Considering worst-case scenarios will help you decide how much funding to have available and for how long.

29. **Be accurate in your forecasting.** Ensure that your forecasts are as accurate as possible. Even if you do not need all of it at once, don't wait until the need for extra financing becomes urgent.

Networking

30. **Seek to help.** To build a strong network for your business, start with people you know. This builds confidence. At every networking opportunity, talk to people, and ask how you could help their business.

31. **Focus on building relationships.** At networking events, seek to build trust and respect instead of just handing out business cards or selling at the first opportunity.

Social Media

32. **It's a social platform to start with.** The basic principle of using social media, as the term implies, is that it is a platform for building relationships with people. The focus should be on building relationships more than direct selling. A suggested ratio is aiming to spend 80 to 90 percent of your time building relationships, and devote the remaining percentage to direct advertising and selling.

33. **Enjoy priceless engagement.** Allow social networking to be an opportunity for feedback and engagement with your content and offerings. Build relationships through patience, depth, integrity, and invaluable experiences with your potential customers.

Benjamin Franklin once said, "*If principle is good for anything, it is worth living up to.*" A business owner's success depends on determination and the ability to adapt and apply time tested proven principles. That is the only way to ensure a profitable return on the time and resources you have invested as well as the success of the business.

In anything you do, success is guaranteed only by the informed steps and actions you take. Wade Hampton said, "*Good principles cannot die,*" and according to Samuel Taylor Coleridge, "*General principles...are to the facts as the root and sap of a tree are to its leaves.*"

Chapter 7

It's Been Done Before

"Opportunities never arrive, they are always seized."
–Pastor Matthew Ashimolowo

———

Every successful enterprise has a story to tell. Allow us to share with you examples of businesses we are all familiar with because of the impact they have made over the years. We highlight how and where they started and how they have evolved to be recognized as international businesses and conglomerates.

Our purpose is to challenge you that business ideas can be inspired by anything.

McDonalds
Dick and Mac McDonald started McDonalds in 1940. They opened the first barbeque restaurant on Fourteenth and E. Street in San Bernardino, California. A few years later, the company began focusing on hamburgers. McDonalds now operates

in 119 countries with 33,500 restaurants worldwide with 2,200 owner/operators in the US alone, serving an estimated 68 million people worldwide. According to the 2011 Annual report and information from its website, McDonalds made $27 billion in sales revenue in 2011, increasing by 2.1% to $27.6 billion in global sales for 2012. What a great example of two people starting a business and zeroing in on a product that resulted in a successful global business.

Nokia

Nokia started as a paper mill in southwestern Finland in 1865. It is now a household name that operates as a global telecommunications leader and connects more than 1.3 billion people worldwide. A quote from Nokia's website states, *"During that time, we've made rubber boots and car tyres. We've generated electricity. We've even manufactured TVs. Changing with the times, disrupting the status quo—it's what we've always done."*

According to Fortune Global 500, Nokia has around 124,800 employees across 120 countries. Net Sales for 2011 was €38.7 billion for sales in 150 countries. Available information on Nokia website reported group turnover for 2012 as €30.2 billion. This company benefited from evolving in product offerings, finding a great niche, and becoming an established business entity.

Kraft Foods

James L. Kraft started his business as a wholesale door-to-door cheese business in Chicago in 1903. He lost $3,000 and a horse in his first year of operation. He was later joined by his four brothers, and they built an international food business. According to their website, Kraft is the "second largest food company in the world with annual revenues of more than $54 billion." It employs an estimated number of 127,000 employees worldwide with consumers in more than 170 countries. Kraft announced its results for the second quarter on August 2, 2012. The company reported 58 cents per share and revenues of $13.29 billion versus the $13.04 billion estimate.

What a grand journey from being a door-to-door cheese business to becoming a global industry leader.

Tesco

Jack Cohen founded Tesco in 1919 when he began to sell surplus groceries from a stall at Well Street Market, Hackney, in the South East of London. The Tesco brand first appeared in 1924. The name came about after Jack Cohen bought a shipment of tea from Thomas Edward Stockwell. He made new labels using the first three letters of the supplier's name (TES), and the first two letters of his surname (CO). The first Tesco store was opened in 1929 in Burnt Oak, Edgware, Middlesex. (*Source: Wikipedia*)

According to its 2011/2012 annual report and Key Facts on the company website, sales revenues came to £72 billion with £3.9 billion profits before tax, with an estimated 500,000 staff operating 6,234 stores worldwide in 13 countries. In its interim results for 2012/2013, Tesco made £36.0 billion in group sales. A remarkable story starting with one person selling surplus goods to locals from a street stall to a company with over 6,000 stores in 14 countries worldwide and an estimated 520,000 employees.

Virgin Group

Sir Richard Branson started his Virgin group of companies, now expanding into 400 companies, with a student magazine called *Student* at the age of 16. He set up an audio record mail-order business in 1970 and then opened a record shop called Virgin Records Shop. The first Virgin Megastore opened on Oxford Street in London. Among his most recent ventures are the Branson Centre of Entrepreneurship in Jamaica, and the world's first purpose-built commercial spaceport, the Galactic Gateway to Space at Spaceport America, was dedicated in 2011. The Galactic Gateway was established to provide the first spaceport built from the ground up to host private enterprise and intended to be the launch of the global commercial spaceflight industry and the second space age.

According to the company website, "The Virgin Group has gone on to grow successful businesses in sectors ranging from mobile telephony, travel, financial services, leisure, music, holidays and health & wellness. Across its companies, Virgin employs approximately 50,000 people, in 34 countries and global branded revenues in 2011 were around £13bn ($21bn)." Who says you have to limit yourself to one industry? From record seller to record label, from hotels and airways to railways and now space travel, Sir Richard Branson has proven that the sky is not the limit.

Sony
In May 1946, Masaru Ibuka started Sony with about twenty dedicated engineers. The original company name was Tokyo Tsushin Kenkyujo. Its first product was a tape recorder, but its breakthrough was the first commercially successful transistor radio, the Sony TR-55.

Sony Corporation has more than thirty subsidiaries in Japan and more than fifty affiliated companies outside of Japan. The affiliate businesses listed on its website range from insurance, banks, and securities to electronics companies. The corporation posted revenues of $81.5 billion for the 2011 fiscal year and $39.3 billion for the fiscal year ending March 31, 2012. This is a great span of diversity for one company. Look around your home, and see what has the Sony symbol on it. It all started from someone opening a post-war business.

Before you dismiss the notion about the relevance of these examples, allow us to highlight a few recent companies that started and have become successful in their own right.

Carol's Daughter

Lisa Price founded Carol's Daughter in 1993 by turning her hobby of mixing fragrances at home into a beauty empire. The company produces more than three hundred products for face, hair, body, and home, with endless product combinations and possibilities. In an interview by Ganeka Gray, for *Clutch Magazine*, July 20, 2009 Price said, "I don't believe I have always had a business mentality—the business began when my mother, Carol, urged me to turn my hobby of making products in my kitchen into a business. So I took $100 and followed my heart and my nose. I made my fragranced oils and body butters, put them in baby food jars and took them down to the church flea market. By the end of that first day, I was pretty much sold out."

Available information from the company's website states, *"Today, we offer prestige hair, body and skincare products made with rare, natural ingredients like Monoi Oil, Shea and Cocoa Butters and Açai. We have collections that repair (top-seller Monoi), perfect curls (classic Hair Milk) and soothe skin (favorite Almond Cookie)."*

A report on March 01, 2012, on Businessweek.com by Susan Decker states, "Carol's Daughter, which now sells its products in standalone stores and in Macy's, has grown to more than 75 employees and is projecting $40 million in revenue this year." Lisa's story exemplifies creativity at its best, turning a hobby into a multimillion-dollar beauty empire.

Kirsty's

Kirsty Henshaw originally had the idea of making ice cream for her son, who had a nut allergy and was wheat-intolerant. She made a dessert with a £30 ice cream machine at her home in Preston, Lancashire in England. However, in 2009, she found a manufacturer and secured £2,500 worth of orders from a health food wholesaler. Her turnover for 2011 came to £550,000. She appeared on the UK start-up show *Dragons' Den* to pitch her business idea to a panel of self-made millionaire business owners and investors. She secured investment of £65,000 from two investors in return for 30 percent share of her allergen-free frozen dessert firm. As at the time of this writing, she has secured a £2 million ready-meal range deal to supply one of the major retail giants, Sainsbury's, in the UK. Henshaw's dairy-free ice cream brand "Freedom" is also due to be launched in the US. Her creativity and drive led her to provide a better solution and healthier alternative, and today she is reaping the rewards.

IROKO Partners

Jason Njoku, the cofounder of IROKO Partners, began his journey in science by obtaining a bachelor's degree in chemistry from the University of Manchester. Njoku shifted gears and began pursing various interests from running a student magazine, financial blog, and a web design venture to owning a t-shirt company. In an interview with TechLoy in April 2012, Njoku shared his story about failure, mistakes, and success. "I spent a good three years making every mistake there was to make about how to run a business," he said. "I ran out of money, I ran out of friends who would lend me money. I was forced to stop." In another interview, he said, "My early failures could have—maybe should have knocked my spirit. But I was determined not to let failure get in the way of raw ambition. I love what I do."

In an interview with Pete Guest of Techloy.com, Guest recalled how Njoku's idea was born. "Apparently, Jason's mother, who he remembers mainly watching British soap operas on TV, was now watching Nolly-wood films on DVD, but finding these movies to buy online wasn't possible and even the stores in London's Brixton Market offered neither an identification of Nollywood films on the movie shelves nor any kind of formalised, organised distribution."

That is when he thought, "this thing seems to be very popular, but there seems to be no distribution around it."

In an article on Blackenterprise.com, Octavia Gordema stated, "It took a trip to Nigeria for Jason Njoku to begin to see success, starting IROKO Partners, the premier source of Nigerian entertainment—from movies to music. After two years of operation, the company has become the world's largest distributor of Nigerian music and movies. IROKO has reached more than 560,000 registered users in less than seven months and has viewers in 178 different countries."

The September 2012 issue of Forbes Africa magazine, in its centrespread titled, "Nigerian Internet maverick and millionaire," featured the following quote: "Every film industry needs a mogul and for Nigeria's film industry, Nollywood, Jason Njoku might just be it." This is classic case of a determined entrepreneur who after much persistence spotted an incredible opportunity to turn his dream into a reality.

Zappos

After an unsuccessful hunt to find a pair of shoes the right size, Nick Swinmurn was inspired to set up Zappos, an online shoe retail business in 1999. By 2007, the company's revenues had grown to more than $800m, increasing to $1 billion in 2008, with more than 1,400 employees. Amazon acquired the firm in 2009. Nick Swinmurn's latest venture is Dethrone, which sells clothing online.

In a Q&A interview with Meghan Cass featured on Zappos.com, Swinmurn said it was a passion for enterprise - not necessarily footwear - got things started. Swinmurn is a prime example of how passion can position someone for opportunity.

Headset.com

In 1997, while running a company in California, Mark Faith became irritated that he couldn't find a reliable supplier of telephone headsets for his offices. After taking it up as a challenge, six weeks later, he went into the headset business. On a BBC interview dated July 15, 2010, when asked his key advice for entrepreneurs and potential business owners, he said, "Look for those things in your life or in your business that annoy you, where you can't get the satisfaction that you want; if you can't find what you want in the market place, and you try hard, it's probably likely there's a business opportunity there." At the time, he had fifty-nine employees and sales turnover of $21 million. Mark Faiths' story demonstrates problem solving at its best. Being a present day solution provider definitely has its rewards.

Innocent Drinks

In 1998, after completion of their university degree, friends Richard Reed, Adam Balon, and Jon Wright obtained jobs, but never stopped talking about setting up a business. Four years later, on their return from a snowboarding holiday, where they spent most of the time talking about their desire to become entrepreneurs, they quit their jobs and decided to go into business. They decided to set up a business that would appeal to people like them, so they fixed on the theme of doing good to themselves. The result was a company that produced pure fruit smoothies, Innocent Drinks. The company now produces more than thirty different recipes and sells more than two million smoothies each week through eleven thousand retailers in 13 different countries. It has an annual turnover of £100 million and employs 250 people.

A BBC News website article stated that, in April 2009, Coca-Cola bought an 18 percent stake in the company for £30 million and a year later paid £65 million for a 58 percent share of the business. Innocent Drink was deemed the official smoothie and juice of the London 2012 Olympic and Paralympics Games. According to the company's website, by committing 10 percent of annual profits towards - Innocent Foundation - to 'do good things', £1.3m has been spent to date, benefiting over 330,000 people directly. The foundation also provides grant for the organization that works with NGOs to deliver their vision of sustainable farming for a secure future. What an inspiring and impactful story of a successful company with passion and charity at heart.

Spanx

At forty-one, Sarah Blakely became the youngest female self-made billionaire in the world. Having failed law school admissions tests twice, she went to work as a meeter-and-greeter for Disney. She then worked as a door-to-door salesperson for an office equipment supplier in Florida and rose to the position of national sales manager. "Blakely's epiphany came when she found she needed a product that didn't yet exist. A sideline in stand-up comedy saw her stuck with what to wear for a show one night. Her white trousers allowed her normal underwear to be seen—the dreaded VPL (visible panty line)." The solution to this wardrobe malfunction was born.

She invested her life savings of $5,000 (£3,190) and the control hosiery, Spanx, was created. She wrote the patent herself to save money.

In 2000, she sent samples to Oprah Winfrey's stylist and received a call from the production company saying that Oprah planned to include Spanx on her "Favorite Things" show. This took Blakely from a single product, sold out of her apartment, to a billion-dollar business.

In 2007, she told Bloomberg Business Week that everything about her journey to get Spanx off the ground entailed having to be a salesperson—from going to the hosiery mills to get a prototype made to calling Saks Fifth Avenue and Neiman Marcus.

Blakely demonstrates how being a solution provider can reap great rewards. She is now part of the elite club of women worth more than a billion dollars.

Gardner Rich

A series of adverse circumstances in the early 1980s left Christopher Gardner homeless and the sole guardian of a toddler son.

According to his biography on Chrisgardnermedia. com, "In 1981, as a new father to son Christopher Gardner Jr., he was determined to find a career that would be both lucrative and fulfilling. Fascinated by finance, but without connections, an MBA or even a college degree, Gardner applied for training programs at brokerages and lived on next to nothing while he learned a new trade. His wife left and Gardner, despite his circumstances, fought to keep his son because, as he says, "I made up my mind as a young kid that when I had children they were going to know who their father is, and that he isn't going anywhere." Gardner worked at Bear Stearns & Co from 1983 to 1987 where he became a top earner. In 1987, he founded the brokerage firm Gardner Rich in Chicago from his home with just $10,000. Gardner Rich LLC is a FINRA registered broker-dealer specializing in servicing public pension funds and Taft-Hartley plans for some of the nation's largest institutions and unions. In addition to expanding its core business as an institutional securities broker, Gardner Rich has increased its participation in corporate underwriting and has expanded its brokerage services to include trading in global markets through both ordinary and ADR form."

Gardener's autobiography, *The Pursuit of Happyness,* became a *New York Times* and *Washington Post* bestseller, and inspired the movie by the same name.

These stories demonstrate how opportunities are identified and creatively nurtured into flourishing businesses. They can inspire you and keep you from disqualifying yourself from becoming a business owner. As the saying goes, *"If you don't know the trees, you may be lost in the forest, but if you don't know the stories, you may be lost in life."* Siberian Elder.

Possibilities still exist, and your level of insight and preparedness to carry a dream through is your key to success in whatever you set yourself to do.

Stories always have a way of relating to us the possibilities that life offers us as a people. If it has been done before, you can do it.

Chapter 8

What's Your Passion?

"Your passion positions you for opportunity and opportunity makes way for success."–**Tonia Askins**

———

If you are passionate about what you do, no obstacle is strong enough to stop you. Although you may start with a seemingly insignificant business idea, as you diligently work at it, it has every potential to expose you to possibilities you would otherwise never have known. The experiences and skills gained boost your confidence to take on daring opportunities that may have seemed daunting when you took the first step. Other business streams could grow from the initial opportunity.

This chapter lists businesses that you can start on a part-time or full-time basis. If you are unemployed or already employed and passionate about a business idea or entertaining the thought of business ownership, you can begin on a part-time basis and as your business grows, make enough to pay yourself and expand to full-time involvement.

We challenge you to not limit yourself to the list.

You could be the next person to innovate a new concept or product that revolutionizes society.

It is also important to understand that certain business opportunities may require experience, education, or certification in the industry.

The likes of Sir Timothy John "Tim" Berners-Lee (inventor of the World Wide Web), Bill Gates (Microsoft), Steve Jobs (co-founder of Apple), Mark Zuckerberg (Facebook), Larry Page and Sergey Brin (Google), and many other tech innovators have provided a huge platform and many tools. When used appropriately, they can help a well-planned and delivered business grow much faster than it would have a few years ago. There is no room to not dream and take your ideas worldwide. Start with an identified opportunity, and create a business that provides solutions to society.

Here are a forty proven businesses that you can start *NOW,* even some on a shoestring budget or limited capital.

1. **Tutoring.** The diverse and ever increasing field of tutoring is a much-needed segment, and it can be started from home or an office. Larger tutoring companies also have opportunities in

various locations for independent representatives and/or franchisees.

2. **Web hosting.** Whether or not you are computer savvy, web hosting reselling is simple to get into passively. You can learn the industry by researching and attending online seminars. Search for hosting reseller opportunities, and compare different plans and resell rates of return to see what best fits.

3. **Real estate investing.** Investing in real estate to create a rental or property selling business may require a high investment in the beginning, but its long-term asset holdings and potential for perpetual income are great. Real estate properties are currently cheaper due to the economic downturn, thus offering more affordable opportunities.

4. **Real estate agenting.** Although becoming a real estate agent doesn't guarantee constant income, it is a good opportunity for part-time earnings until your portfolio grows to a substantial level. If you enjoy learning about real estate, this will be a great fit.

5. **Marketing consulting.** Assisting business owners reach their goals through marketing and advertising platforms is great for someone who loves to promote other businesses. A person with experience in advertising or marketing can take advantage of this opportunity. Due to the

vastness of social media outlets, opportunities for marketing and advertising consulting have vastly increased.

6. **Courier services.** Opportunities in this industry vary according to your location. Many businesses such as flower shops, restaurants, and gift shops rely on courier services to deliver products. Some courier businesses also transport documents and packages for individuals, businesses, and institutions. Most operate in daytime hours, but night and evening opportunities also exist.

7. **Limousine services.** Special occasions usually demand special transportation. There are a couple affordable ways to start out within this industry. One option is to offer your services as a sub-contracting driver for an existing company. Another option is to lease or buy from an existing company that may own a fleet of limousines or a dealer.

8. **Maintenance and repair.** If you're good with household fixtures and appliances this may be the opportunity for you. Consider starting by offering your services to neighbors or friends and family, and then network and call large service companies, offering your services as a subcontractor. The amount of the project and scope of work usually determines whether licensing is required. Check your local build-

ers' organization for current regulations and possible opportunities.

9. **Grant writing.** Grant writers are an invaluable resource and are usually hired by nonprofit organizations to assist in securing funding opportunities. You can find classes, books, and other resources, ranging from the beginner to advanced level, to study this industry. The tough economy has indeed taken a toll on nonprofits, so good grant writers have become more valuable to organizations to remain and obtain much needed funding.

10. **Travel tour operation.** As long as people need to get away from home, there will be a need for tour operators. If you reside near busy cities, the demand is usually greater, but there are opportunities in more rural areas as well. If you're in a historical area, learn about its history and culture. If you're passionate enough about this field, you can create your own tours. Most visitors bureaus have a tremendous amount of free literature that you can use to begin.

11. **Business associations.** If you're a professional or keenly knowledgeable in a specific area of business, social, and enjoy helping others, this may be the business for you. Associations provide businessmen and women from every field new networking platforms. Because of the advances in technology, it is easier than

ever to create an association platform that you are passionate about. You can offer members opportunities for mentorship, social events, education, and business partnering.

12. **Car washing.** This is a fun and exciting business to start and can be very lucrative. As long as busy individuals have cars, there will be a need for such services. Car wash businesses are not limited to the standard, standalone car wash; to add revenue to the bottom line some offer personalized services such as home service and luxury car detailing.

13. **Jewelry making.** Opportunities in the jewelry industry depend on levels of skill or interest such as designing, manufacturing, and handcrafting and/or selling ready-made jewelry. You can earn additional revenue in this industry by providing services such as adjusting, repairing, cleaning, polishing, appraising, and teaching.

14. **Agents and managers.** If you have experience in a particular industry and enjoy negotiating contracts and brokering business partner relationships, consider becoming an agent for others in the field.

15. **Writing.** Are you good with words? Do you have experience writing for a newspaper or magazine? Developing original content for online platforms and entities could be the start-up business for you. Platforms in this field include

advertisements, books, magazines, film and television scripts, and songs. One of the latest opportunities for writers is working with web publishers who need new content to enhance the site visitor's experience.

16. **Independent arts.** Opportunities for independent artist vary as much as the industry itself. Craft artists create handmade objects such as pottery, glassware, or other objects for practical use. Fine artists, including illustrators, painters, and sculptors, create original works of art for artistic and visual value rather than a practical purpose. The products can be sold independently, wholesale, or via other methods of distribution.

17. **Graphic design.** Graphic designers can specialize in design, publishing, or advertising and related services. If you have graphic design software experience and/or education, this will be a great start-up for you. Graphic designers are sought out for virtually every type of creative concept design you see around, ranging from various types of projects including - logos, billboards, website designs and countless others.

18. **Daycare.** There are great part-time business opportunities for those who love being with children. The opportunities are vast due to the demands on working parents and families. The only caveat is, you may need to apply for license and pass background checks.

19. **Home organizing.** Due to time constraints, many people need help keeping things in the home in order. Starting off, home organizers can work as subcontractors or partner affiliates with established companies. Within this industry, there are even certifications to help solidify you and your skills as you grow your business and clientele.

20. **Special events coordinating.** This is an exciting and demanding business, therefore don't take it on lightly. Many people invest heavily in special events. You should be detailed oriented, a good project manager, and able to organize and plan events. To learn about the field, request internship opportunities or volunteer with established event management companies.

21. **Cake designing.** Cake designing is a great way to use your skills if you love baking and pastry making or have experience making specialized cakes. Classes are offered to enhance skills in cake decorating and design at community vocational schools and universities.

22. **Home cleaning.** Who doesn't need a house cleaner? With this business opportunity, you can price your service however you see fit to make a profit and fill demand. Remember, as in any business, create unique selling points that set you apart from others.

23. **Pressure washing.** Home and business support services such as pressure washers are needed by homeowners and businesses to remove loose grime, dust, and dirt from surfaces and objects. Such cleaning support services are always in demand and providing a quality pressure washing service within your city would be a great part-time start-up. With pressure washing, you can start by operating your business on the weekends and expand from there.

24. **Pet support.** Most pet owners need pet grooming, sitting and walking services. If you love pets, this business is worth considering.

25. **Self-enrichment education.** Opportunities exist to instruct in a variety of disciplines. You can teach subjects that students take for fun or self-improvement such as piano lessons, foreign languages, gymnastics, or cooking.

26. **Translation.** Sourcing your language skills as an interpreter or translator is a great option for a part-time business. Opportunities can be found in schools, courtrooms, business corporations, media houses, publishers, embassies, consulates, as well as diplomatic missions. Many translators also have the option of working from home.

27. **Travel booking.** Travel agents organize, sell, and offer advice on destinations packages, plan itineraries, and make travel arrangements for

businesses and individuals. This industry also has subcontracting opportunities with larger firms. If you love travel and enjoy people, this may be the field for you. At certain levels of operation, you may need some form of certification.

28. **Medical transcription.** Medical transcriptionists are needed for practically every physicians report. They listen to voice recordings that health professionals make and convert them into written transcripts for the patient files. They can work from home and be independently contracted.

29. **Notary public.** Notaries provide assistance in a range of legal services: powers-of-attorney, legalization of documents, vehicle title transfers, business contracts, administration of oaths and affirmations, affidavits, and statutory declarations. Practices allowed differ by jurisdiction. Check with your local bar association about duties, responsibilities, and privileges. This is a great business for "legal eagles" or those with knowledge and interest in the legal field.

30. **Office administration.** If you're great at multitasking and secretarial duties, this is the business for you. Individuals and businesses need office administrators to organize files, draft messages, help write resumes, and schedule meetings and events. Businesses

facing financial distress are having problems keeping full-time secretarial staff and are keen to outsource this service to private administrative service providers. If a company hires you for such a service, it usually does so on a contractual basis (without benefits), thus reducing the employer's expenditures.

31. **Restaurant consulting.** Experience and the right certification in restaurant management and/or food safety can be a great asset in providing consulting services to the fast-paced restaurant industry. Look for opportunities to provide such services to restaurants in your city or metropolitan area. As in any consultancy business, the level of your expansion depends on how beneficial and profitable your services are to your clients.

32. **Landscaping.** This field is perfect for plant lovers and experienced groundskeepers. A landscape specialist plans, organizes, directs, or coordinates landscaping or grounds keeping services. This could include planting and maintaining trees, flowers, and lawns, depending on the contract.

33. **Security.** If you have a background in law enforcement, are physically fit, and are interested in providing security services, this is the perfect business for you. There are many opportunities in this industry including

entertainment (protection for high-profile individuals and celebrities), public and private properties, retail outlets, and gaming centers. The requirements depend on the location, level of security needed, and setting.

34. **Tax preparing.** Thank goodness for those who take the stress out of tax preparation. You can start a tax preparation service after taking a few courses. Major tax firms and accredited tax bodies, as well as local colleges, provide such courses. Many individuals and small businesses need assistance in filing tax returns on a regular basis.

35. **Answering service.** An answering service business is great for someone with experience in call center, multiline switchboard, or secretarial services. Professionalism, flexibility, attention to detail, and efficiency are the key attributes needed for this low-cost start up.

36. **Private detective services.** Private detectives find out information about legal, financial, and personal matters. They offer services to businesses and individuals such as verifying a person's background, tracing missing persons, and investigating computer crimes. Some also double as high-profile security and protect individuals and celebrities.

37. **Personal training.** Do you love challenging others to be physically fit? Personal trainers

have clients ranging from stay-at-home parents to "A list" celebrities. Due to the high awareness of the benefits of leading a healthy life, this industry has experienced a real boost in recent times. Additional revenue can be earned by creating books, videos, and other proprietary products.

38. **Personal chef/catering.** Do you enjoy cooking, and do others enjoy your cooking? With the time constraints on families, it is worthwhile to consider becoming a personal chef. You can also be hired for events such as wedding receptions, birthday parties, and movie sets.

39. **Photography.** You can start in this industry with little or no investment. Your creativity, coupled with a good photogenic sense and willingness to learn, can help you become a distinguished photographer. Opportunities also exist for you to license or sell your works to individuals or businesses, showcase them at exhibitions, create catalogues, books, and publish your work through various media outlets.

40. **Blogging.** You can create a niche blog by writing about unique products, industries, events, and subjects. Your particular writing style can be a distinguishing feature in the presentation of the subject matter. The basis for a good blogging business is your ability to excite your followers and keep them coming back. It provides

you with the opportunity to find creative ways of monetizing your site.

Reports from international research and consulting companies such as IBIS World, McKinsey & Company, Technomic Consulting, and Plunkett Research confirm that most of the opportunities highlighted above have great potential for growth. Refer to Appendix IV for highlights of some of the research from the above companies.

The list of business stories and market data is inexhaustive. Even during "oversaturation" of an industry (when too many businesses offer the same products or services), a new business with the right knowledge and strategy can enter the market and compete effectively by offering better value, excellent service, innovative pricing and promotional strategies. Being creative in strategies of business, challenges you to think outside the standard way of getting things done.

A complete new business idea, concept or product can always be introduced into the right market.

The ideas for new products or services are always lurking in someone's mind, needing to be introduced. In the words of Richard Branson, founder of Virgin Enterprises, *"Business opportunities are like buses, there's always another one coming."*

Chapter 9

Successful Systems

"Organize around business functions, not people. Build systems within each business function. Let systems run the business and people run the systems. People come and go but the systems remain constant"
–Michael Gerber

———

As highlighted in chapter 6, it is very important to start your business with an operational system in mind. A successful business system should not be confused with a business model. What we refer to as a successful business system is how various aspects of the business interact, are operated and coordinated day-to-day.

A successful business system ensures the following:

- Offers you a structured platform you can easily build on.
- Provides you with the freedom and ease to train others to operate the business even without your direct day-to-day involvement.

- Makes it possible for you to confidently entrust your trained employees to manage the business while you focus on other important areas such as networking and building strategic partnerships for growth and expansion.
- Enables you to easily identify what is working and what needs to be changed.
- Becomes the basis for your organizational policies.
- Helps you to expand your operations as you get to the stage to branch out.
- Helps you to license your growing business to others as a franchise.
- Inspires you to branch out into other lines of trade different from what you originally set up to deliver.

What constitutes a successful system? Given the complexities of the types of businesses that exist or are yet to be created, we believe that every business should have the following core systems in place or at least have them in mind from the start to develop and build on. They are essential if you want to stay in business for the long haul.

- **Operations overview.** You need a written plan of the system you are creating. In it, you can articulate the structure of your system for others to study understand and follow. It serves as a guide for managing the business, or a section of it, when employees are entrusted with the responsibility. A good business plan can form the basis of the development of these sets of systems. However, an operational system overview will be an internal document and will include the detailed structure, order, requirements, responsibilities, and duties required for the day-to-day operations and management of the business.

- **Administration.** An administrative system must be in place to manage the business documentation, office setup, and electronic and non-electronic correspondence. Although workspaces vary according to professions and needs, and whether based in a home or an acquired office space, the basics are the same. For instance, a lawn service business won't need the same office setup as a freelance artist, but the fundamentals are essentially the same. The main thing to keep in mind is that if you decide to have a home business, homes were not set up to be commercial space, so creativity and practical planning are important.

The administrative system orders and structures the office setup as a whole, coordinating all aspects of the business. It includes such functions as filing, furnishing, and management of inventory, email, mail, time and organizing of tasks throughout a workday. The administrative system also coordinates the departments of the business and allocates responsibilities to employees and management. A qualified office manager or administrator is usually responsible for managing this system.

- **Human resources.** An HR system is needed to manage processes related to past, current and potential employees. Such a system outlines the interviewing, hiring, and termination processes, ensuring regulatory compliance, assessing the appropriate time to hire an employee, determining what skill sets and qualifications are necessary for positions, identifying of the best media to use in finding the right candidates, establishing salary levels, outlining the responsibilities of staff, creating an organization holiday schedule, forming policies concerning employee performance, and setting out the organization's structure, vision, and hierarchy. An HR manager is often tasked with the responsibility of coordinating this system and often times collaborate with others in management pending the matter.

- **Bookkeeping.** Until you can hire a qualified finance manager or a professional accountant, it is important to have a bookkeeping system in place to organize the business's financial transactions. These include purchases, sales, receipts, and payments made by individuals on behalf of the organization. A good bookkeeping system enables qualified accountants to easily create reports from the financial transactions recorded by the designated staff member trained to do the bookkeeping or a hired bookkeeper. You can get basic training in bookkeeping to enable you to carry out this function at the start of the business, thus saving you the cost of hiring a bookkeeper or paying an accountant to take over that responsibility. However, as the business grows, you may need to hire a bookkeeper to take over this responsibility. You could also contract an accounting firm to manage the bookkeeping, creation of financial reports, and filling of returns with the respective agencies.

- **Marketing.** Establishing a marketing system means clearly identifying your target market and knowing where to find it and how to access it. This system also helps you to identify the best media or platforms to make your products and services known to your target market. You will need to develop an advertising strategy to create the awareness that generates sales.

- **Sales.** A sales system outlines strategic approaches for selling your products to prospective customers. This includes what aspects of your product or service to emphasize while engaging potential clients. (In chapter 6, we discussed the need to always seek to identify and highlight the benefit of your product or service to prospects.) Other aspects include, knowing strategically tested methods necessary to close a deal and how to follow up for repeat business and referrals. When creating a sales system the importance of repeat business and up-selling or add-on selling during opportune times are aspects that you definitely do not want to overlook.

- **Credit.** It is essential to have a system in place if you intend to offer some or all aspects of your business services or products on credit. The system should include determining whether a client or customer qualifies for credit, the quantity or service levels at which you allow credit, the trade or cash discounts allowed to encourage swift payments or bulk buying, when to require payment, and what to do in the event of delays and defaults. The key is a system that enables credit to work to your advantage while offering the customers a convenient means of payment.

- **Debt management.** A debt management system is necessary to ensure that the lifeblood of the business—cash—is not drained. A good debt management system will establish how much a customer can owe the business, the number of days it has to repay the debt (whether in stages or as a one-time payment), procedures to monitor the debt and follow up to ensure prompt payment, how to deal with late payments, and methods to recover funds from defaulted customers. This system is too important to be ignored.

- **Customer care.** A good customer care system should align the business offering with customer needs at every level, not just what you like, want to sell, or how convenient it is to deliver your products and services. A business that displays its products to the public and potential customers should set up its stores with convenience and a good customer experience in mind. All staff members need to be adequately trained to employ the right approach in interacting with customers and potential customers. A system should be set in place to deal with customer queries, complaints, and feedback. For instance, dealing with customer complaints is too important to be left to staff without the necessary authority to resolve the issue.
- **Supplier.** Any business with a constant need for supplies in producing its products or services must have a workable supplier system to ensure smooth operations. This system includes criteria for identifying the best supplier that is in line with how the organization likes to function. It also includes, credit terms

where necessary or available, identifying the quality or grade of supplies needed, the stock levels based on your organization's storage capacity as well as reorder levels, and alternative suppliers, should your first-choice suppliers fail to meet orders or go out of business.

- **Payment.** A payment system is essential to organize payments received from customers, payments to suppliers, salaries, wages, and any other benefits due to employees. This system manages the payment process from the point of sale, how and when to deposit daily proceeds and record them to keep track of cash flow. Payment to suppliers involve taking into account credit terms and organizing payments on due dates to avoid incurring charges. You can pay on time to take advantage of discount incentives that may be on offer. In regards to payment for employee payroll, benefits and taxes, you have the choice to outsource, utilize payroll software, or manually complete it. In all cases, a successful system should clearly identify the employees authorized and responsible for managing the payment systems at different levels. You should also have a system in place to handle customer refunds, should there be a need for them.

In creating a system, it is equally important to be clear on the processes involved in operating it. In the words of W. Edwards Deming, *"if you can't describe what you are doing as a process, you don't know what you're doing."*

Although there could be other systems to ensure the smooth day-to-day operation of the business, we recommend those listed here as a great starting point. For a new business owner, managing all these systems may not be possible at first. Develop them gradually and allocate various tasks for different hours of the day or days of the workweek. For instance, some small business owners allocate the first hour or two of the day to email and correspondence, work on products or projects in the mid-afternoon, do filing in late afternoon, and catch up on industry news and complete reporting work towards the end of the day.

An existing business can equally adopt these set of recommended systems to fully benefit from their advantages. As mentioned,

Having good business systems in place provides a strong foundation and the proper course for your business in any given industry to grow and expand.

Chapter 10

Progress With Right Connections

"None of us is as smart as all of us."–**Ken Blanchard**

—⚬—

As in life, progress is necessary for survival and fulfilment. Make progress even if you feel it is slow—you are further along than you were yesterday.

> *Eliminate doubt, and do not succumb to the time factor that is common among start-ups.*

Here are five ways to stay on course.

Be Steady

Going steady with your business will involve, firmly committing the time it takes to develop it. Be determined to be your best, and never lose sight of your ultimate goals and objectives. If you want a mental picture of what it means to be steady, think about a woman on a tightrope. She's focused, calm, fixed, and committed to finish. She gets across at a balanced and steady pace.

Stay Consistent

Consistency is an important principle. Think about the best restaurant or place you often visit. What makes you return? You expect the same thing, if not better, whether it's the food or the service. It got you to return. This is what you want your customer base to feel about your products or services.

Work in Progress

Even at its peak, an established business will put itself at risk by resting on its past success. Despite any level of success achieved, make every effort to improve on your products, and strive to capture market share through continued strategic progress.

Reinvest in Yourself

As you progress, continue to improve your craft and skills. Continuous improvement greatly enhances your confidence and offerings to your consumers. Even when you have achieved a client base that's in line with your targets or expectations, continued investment in yourself will keep you on your toes and positions you to compete effectively. There are a variety of ways to enhance your existing skills or add complimentary skills to your portfolio.

Keep in mind that when you add a new skill, depending on your business, it has the potential to become an additional service offering and boost revenues.

For example, Paula opened a tax service in a local retail mall. While driving home one day, she spotted a banner advertising that the community college offered classes to become a notary. She knew that certification as a notary could be a new specialized service niche for her business. In addition to becoming a new revenue stream, offering new services are smart as long as it does not conflict but enhance your core services.

Reinvesting in yourself produces an energy that trickles down in your business and reinvigorates your flow to grow. It also means taking care of your most basic needs - resting, eating properly, and exercising go a long way in functioning effectively.

Stay on pace, and consistently apply your acquired knowledge and new tools to accomplish your objectives.

One of the most beneficial things you can do is learn from the experience of others by way of connecting with a strategic set of people to learn and grow even faster.

Make the Right Connections
To start, grow and profit in business, developing the right connections is vitally important.

As fellow entrepreneurs, we know that often, especially in the first few years, you need some motivational boosters and fresh ideas to sail through momentary stormy periods. We challenge you to reach out and connect with others. Locate a trustworthy entrepreneur, business mentor, advisor, or coach who can assist you on your journey. Reaching out does not have to be only face-to-face meetings. Sometimes you will have to connect with fellow entrepreneurs through books, networks, seminars, or social media.

Developing the right connections means joining appropriate networks. Most networks are created as platforms for individuals with common interests to assist each other in their growth and development. Using today's technology, most networks are just a click away, and you will find different industry network platforms as well as those that provide specific platforms for mentorships. Joining them will afford you the opportunity to meet people who inspire you to go the extra mile, empower you, and offer you insight about the situations you may encounter as a business owner. As you make new connections remember to give credit to those who made significant impact on your journey.

While connecting, remain genuinely positive and focus on learning and sharing.

1. Be you: Stay true to your core.
2. Stay positive: Don't be an energy zapper.
3. Learn: Be open to suggestions.

4. Grow: Don't allow personal prejudice to interfere.
5. Acknowledge: Honor those who help you along the way.
6. Share: Be there for others.

Many entrepreneurs neglect the last two points. Acknowledgment can be given in various forms, according to the level of impact: a referral, a thank you, or a supportive action will keep the flow of reciprocity going, depending on what you feel is appropriate. Give back to others. Benjamin Disraeli said, *"The greatest good you can do for another is not just to share your riches but to reveal to him his own."*

When you come across new business owners who ask for help, offer a tip or two in the appropriate setting, they may be exceptionally grateful. You will get busy with your business, and you may forget that someone else is in the position today that you were in the past. *"Be an opener of doors for such as come after thee, and do not try to make the universe a blind alley,"* said Ralph Waldo Emerson. Continue to help others as often as you have the opportunity. Winston Churchill once said, *"We make a living by what we get, but we make a life by what we give."*

Chapter 11

The Business Life Cycle

"What is destructive is impatience, haste, expecting too much too fast."–**May Sarton**

———

To go into business for yourself is an exciting experience, and at the same time, business owners may become their own "worst enemy" by expecting too much too soon. Many of us seem to overlook the fact that for every established business, there is a story behind its success or continued existence. The business success stories are the result of years of persistence, hard and smart work, adjustments, changes, fine tuning ideas and systems, with sometimes-near bankruptcy experiences. All of which help to define the business we are familiar with and patronize for products and services.

> *Success in business is not determined by just one large order or sale, but by cumulative events that enable a business to manage its structure, profitability and growth for the foreseeable future.*

Drawing on our cumulative business experience of more than thirty-five years, we believe that most if not all businesses go through cycles. Here we highlight the stages entrepreneurs go through when they aspire to start a business and drive it to become a market leader. It's not a must that every business goes through all the stages. However, understanding the stages will be helpful in managing your expectations as you start and grow a successful business.

This is the pictorial view of the business life cycle, and an explanation of each stage follows.

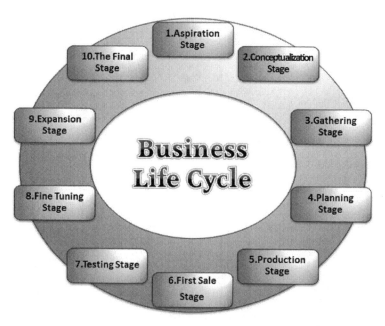

1. **Aspiration.** At this stage, you consider starting a business and are sold on the idea but have yet

to identify which direction to go. While some people have had such an aspiration from childhood, others are forced to consider the idea because of unemployment or underemployment. Some are also inspired by stories, thoughts provoking books such as this one, entrepreneurship drive initiatives, as well as other reasons we may never know.

2. **Conceptualization**. At this stage, you have identified an opportunity or idea you want to pursue. This could include being inspired by the business opportunities we have highlighted in this book, being motivated by other businesses or by developing your passion, experience and skills into a business venture.

3. **Gathering**. This stage makes a huge difference between succeeding and failing. It's at this stage you research the idea, seek advice, and narrow down the options for moving forward. Your success largely depends on how much time and resources you invest in research and how you strategically utilize the information gathered to start.

4. **Planning**. At this stage, you draw up a structured plan or business plan, using all the information gathered. The organization's mission and objectives should form the basis of the plan. The act of planning helps you to think things through thor-

oughly, study and research further if you are not sure of the facts, and look at your ideas critically.

5. **Production**. It is at this stage you pull together your resources to create products ready for potential customers. The production process begins for your first set of products, and service packages are put together and made available to consumers.

6. **First sale.** This is when the "first fruits" of the business are purchased, and customers part with their cash for the products and/or services of the business. It's fulfilling and a first leg of achievement for any business.

7. **Testing.** By this stage, the business systems and operations are put to the test. The amount of testing at this stage depends on the volume of business, complexity of systems and operations, and the business environment or challenges the business faces. Testing could take a couple of months to three years or more.

8. **Fine Tuning.** The business at this stage seeks out ways to alter, correct or fine-tune operations to establish the best methods and practices. Adopting measures necessary to improve its systems, products, and services to become a better and excellent business. Businesses that pass this stage are more certain to be successful for the long haul, as long as it keeps improving and adapting to business trends.

9. **Expansion**. This is the stage where the business has already defined its systems and methods and is ready to duplicate itself by branching out or franchising. It has achieved success with established systems for smooth operations, consistently made profits, and grown beyond its first operational site or store. Other business owners may choose to license the brand, model, and systems as a franchise.

10. **Final stage.** The business has become a major player in its industry and has the potential to become a market leader. Not many businesses get to this stage. Those who do must have established themselves as a reputable brand and been in business for a significant number of years, which could be up to an average of ten years. The business still needs to innovate, adapt to changing consumer needs and trends, and adopt advances in technology to stay ahead of the game.

We challenge aspiring entrepreneurs to follow their dreams and passion in making the best of whatever circumstances they face and from where they are in life. We are equally mindful of the fact that however, you decide to pursue your dreams, managing expectations is too important to ignore. Many give up on their way to fulfilling a dream because of the high expectations they had and their unwillingness to make room for unexpected delays and events that could crop up. Thus, denying them of the golden prize of success they so craved for.

With that in mind, wisely manage your expectations of success so that you don't give up due to discouragement or loss of confidence. Success is achievable irrespective of challenges or a seemingly sluggish pace of growth. In the words of Pastor Matthew Ashimolowo, President and Senior Pastor of Kingsway International Christian Centre, "*Success is a product of over time not overnight.*"

Chapter 12

Conclusion

"Do not think it impossible just because it has never happened."–**Stephen R. Lawhead**

———

It has been an interesting journey sharing practical information, valuable tools and experienced based knowledge, with the hope and expectation of helping you turn challenging situation you may face into a secured future. Whether you are unemployed, under-employed, completed high school, earned a doctorate, are a stay- at- home mom or dad, professional woman or man on the go or just want to earn extra income, we trust that this book will be an invaluable resource on your journey to a secured successful future.

We also hope that the systems, principles and inspiring examples will encourage and equip current business owners, those facing challenges, on the verge of bankruptcy or those that may have closed down due to the uncertain economic climate.

We have been there and understand how testing the journey can be. We also recognise that it can become an opportune life-changing experience you might never have encountered, had it not been for the challenges.

As we compared notes, we realized how interestingly similar our journeys have been, although we are from different continents and professional backgrounds. We have also encountered similar stories that clients and participants have shared from our seminars and individual consultations. Our driving force is the desire to lend our experience, inspire and help you appreciate that there is still hope, while realistically addressing your situation to creatively turn it around to your advantage.

It is equally important to take informed actionable steps to realize your full economic potential.

Our philosophy is rooted in this Latin proverb: *"If the wind will not serve, take to the oars."* In other words, if circumstances around you are not favourable to spur you on, take the reins and chart your course. *"You do not need to know precisely what is happening, or exactly where it is all going. What you need is to recognize the possibilities and challenges offered by the present moment, and to embrace them with courage, faith and hope,"* said Thomas Merton.

The journey starts in your mind, and that is also where your dream can possibly be shelved or excused.

Nothing else can limit what you can do or how far you can go. Start the journey with a persistent positive mind set to turn around any adverse circumstance into a lasting, successful experience. In the words of Babe Ruth, *"Never let the fear of striking out get in your way."*

We have also researched and shared the stories of those who started businesses and explored the diverse angles by which they did so and became successful. There are countless millions who are equally successful in their businesses worldwide; and every product, service, or concept out there has a story behind it.

To start a business and succeed is possible, doable and achievable.

It is as simple as that. However, between starting and becoming successful, you need to skilfully make the right decisions and work smart, employing the right tools and resources. We despise poverty and believe in creating wealth by tapping into your passion, experience, skills, creativity and opportune market conditions. Whatever you do, *"Never forget that money is stored energy that allows us freedom to do what we want with our lives,"* said Allan Roth.

Now is the time for action. Make up your mind that there is no time to sit and do nothing. The time has come to channel your passion to identify the opportunities on which you can capitalize. With the time-tested business principles shared in this book, you can start smart and be ahead of the game from the onset.

> *Do the right thing, in the right way at the right time, and you will reap the right results on your way to a successful future.*

You are on course to creating a business in line with your passion. Napoleon Hill said, *"Desire is the starting point of all achievement, not a hope, not a wish, but a keen pulsating desire which transcends everything."* In the quest to a financially independent life, success is achievable when you take advantage of the right knowledge.

We also challenge you to never "take your eye off the ball." Having a clear-cut understanding and appreciation of the rewards you stand to gain by charting an entrepreneurial course will get you through the journey. That is why we dedicated a chapter to the benefits of going into business for yourself. It has been said that, *"winners visualize the rewards of success, whereas losers visualize the penalties of failure."*

We have also highlighted how success demands smart actions and the right level of knowledge. The question is, how determined are you to succeed, irrespective of what challenges you are facing right now? Richard B.

Sheridan, the playwright and former long-term owner of the London Theatre Royal, once said, *"The surest way not to fail is to determine to succeed."*

The time is now. The pathway to succeeding as an entrepreneur starts with the steps you take in turning the rich contents of this book into a passion-driven, problem solving money-making venture. Our ultimate desire is your success.

It is not over, you can creatively turn this around.

Appendix I

Below are some of the news stories that reflect the nature of the dramatic changes in the economies of the world.

"*Implementing austerity measures too quickly will send ailing Euro zone economies into a "downward spiral,"* US President Barack Obama warned on Friday adding that, *an European recession would harm the pace of the US recovery.*" Telegraph News website - June 8, 2012.

"*British Prime Minister David Cameron on Thursday warned German Chancellor Angela Merkel that the euro is at risk without decisive action from Berlin. The British Premier came to the German capital with a message that Merkel must move quickly to save the single currency's stricken economies.*" Euro News website – June 7, 2012.

A CNN Money website article by Mark Thompson on November 7, 2012 indicated, "*The Center for Economics and Business Research said Monday it expects the euro zone to remain in recession throughout 2013 – shrinking by 0.4 percentage point -- and return to only marginal growth the following year. In the same article, the* chief executive of CEBR was quoted as saying, *"The economic situation in some parts of Europe is moving from bad to catastrophic,"*

A Reuters US edition news website by Ellen Freilich on Nov 15, 2012, stated, *"Global stocks fell for a seventh day on Thursday after data showed the Euro zone entered a recession in the third quarter and on fear of the U.S. "fiscal cliff," while oil prices declined despite a flare-up of violence in the Gaza Strip."*

How about this direct and frank admission from China?

"Mr. Wen and other Chinese officials at the International Monetary Fund (IMF) warned last week that a recession in Europe could halve China's growth rates." BBC website – February 14, 2012

Appendix II

Here are some unemployment statistical data that reflects the nature of the dramatic changes in the employment conditions around the globe. The examples further underscore how intertwined and uncertain the world economies have become.

The latest unemployment data indicates that the US unemployment rate was 7.9 percent at the end of October 2012, edged down to 7.8 percent in November while remaining unchanged at 7.8 percent in December (US Bureau of Labor Statistics website – January 4, 2013). Among countries covered by the BLS international comparisons program, Italy (11.10 percent) and France (10.3 percent) had the highest unemployment rates. For Canada, the unemployment rate decreased to 7.10 percent in December of 2012 from 7.20 percent in November of 2012, according to Statistics Canada, January 2013.

On the other hand, "The unemployment rate dropped to 7.8 percent of the economically active population for July - September 2012, down 0.1 on the quarter in the UK. There were 2.51 million unemplo people, down 49,000 on the quarter," and it remained unchanged at 7.80 percent in October of 2012 from 7.80 percent in September 2012, according to UK Office of National Statistics December 12, 2012.

Eurostat reported January 8, 2013, the eurozone unemployment rate hit a record high at 11.8% in November from 11.6 percent in September, with 18.8m people out of jobs. The highest were in Spain at 25.02 percent. That of Australia rather decreased to 5.20 percent in November of 2012 from 5.30 percent in October of 2012, according to Australian Bureau of Statistic.

In addition, in its 2013 Global Employment Trends report, the ILO forecasts unemployment numbers to rise by 5.1 million in 2013 to reach 202 million, rising further in 2014 to reach 205 million. In an interview with CNBC, Ekkehard Ernst, chief of the employment trends unit at the ILO said, *"Unemployment remains as dire as it was during the crisis in 2009."*

Appendix III

Below are a few figures representing the number of start-ups for the US and UK.

According to the Kauffman Index of Entrepreneurial Activity, in 2009, 558,000 individuals took the decision and started new businesses in the US, 4 percent more than in 2008. It also said, "Rather than making history for its deep recession and record unemployment, 2009 might instead be remembered as the year business start-ups reached their highest level in 14 years—even exceeding the number of start-ups during the peak 1999–2000 technology boom." In 2010, the foundation reported that 565,000 new businesses were started in the United States.

The October 13, 2010 BBC News website ran an article that stated, "The number of new businesses set up in the UK during the first six months of 2010 was the highest amount in more than a decade. A total of 204,361 new firms were established during the period, said business support group Yoodoo, which analyzed Companies House (the UK body responsible for registering a business) data."

In January 2012, figures released by intelligence supplier Creditsafe website, indicated that "close to half a million small firms were set up in 2011" in the United Kingdom. Research by the national enterprise campaign further showed that in 2012 484,224 businesses were started, compared to 440,600 in 2011. Emma Jones, co-founder of StartUp Britain said: *"These figures are hot off the press, they are unaudited at the moment, but what it's telling us is that there was a clear increase in start-up rates in 2012.*

Appendix IV

The following research data support some of the available sectors with great potential for growth and opportunities for start-ups.

As more people flock to e-commerce websites, demanding customized goods and the ability to compare prices, opportunities in this sector grow rapidly. In the United States, according to Plunkett Research, travel sales grew by 16 percent in 2012. It is projected to reach $125 billion by the end of the 2012, and the number of businesses in the industry is expected to grow from 52,969 to more than 61,000 over the next five years. A focus on customization and localization will be a big selling point for a new business.

Although restaurant businesses experienced some decline at the height of the economic downturn, healthy eating continues to remain popular, especially when a restaurant offers locally sourced and locally grown foods, according to the US National Association of Restaurants. A report by a food-service research and consulting firm, Technomic, indicated that the biggest trend for 2012 will be meals with a twist—"comfort food" with an ethnic spin or surprising tweaks to sandwiches.

With the increase in the use of smartphones and tablets, the mobile gaming industry has experienced a huge increase in the last couple of years. According to Plunkett Research, the industry has seen a growth in yearly app downloads of 30 percent, and 13 billion apps are projected to be downloaded in 2012. IBIS World projects this industry to generate $4.5 billion in revenues and expects it to rise to $12.3 billion by 2017. A concept that stands out and generates excitement is a great way forward. The huge user-base platform offered by Facebook, for instance, has enabled app companies to earn millions of dollars for their creations as well as massively earning from acquisitions and mergers. In 2011, for instance, Electronic Arts bought PopCap Games, maker of Bejeweled and Plants vs. Zombies, for $750 million.

Authors Biography

Tonia Askins

Entrepreneur and International Business Consultant, has serviced individuals, emerging entrepreneurs, existing small business owners and corporations for over fifteen years. Her client list ranging from Fine Artists to Computer Application Developers is just as diverse as her experience. Right from LSU Tonia's management and executive career took-off, gaining industry experience within – mortgage finance, law, real estate and hospitality. Tonia has also success-fully managed and administered an international non-profits human resources department overseeing more than 100 employees, operating within – group benefits, employee relations, recruitment, and non-profit law. An entrepreneur at heart, she founded the US based firms, Virtual Live Assistant and Northstar Pathways Consulting and Coaching, offering vari-ous executive, management and administrative busi-ness support services globally. Her other experience includes owning and managing a restaurant. Tonia is also the founder of Louisiana Love, a special events photography company which provides photography for a national publisher as well as covers major events by request for arts, entertainment and humanitarian efforts within Louisiana. Service through volunteering to non-profits and individuals through mentoring and coaching has provided some of her most rewarding efforts. Truly, a no limits mind-set, diverse experience and passion for people are her main driving force.

Victor Kwegyir

Is an international business consultant, business motivational speaker, author, the founder and CEO of Vike Invest (UK) Ltd, a growing International Business Consultancy firm in London, UK. He has over fifteen years experience in business, and holds a Masters degree (MSc in International Financial Systems) with other qualifications. He speaks internationally at seminars, challenging and equipping people with the knowledge and practical tools in starting and growing a successful business. Victor is a regular guest speaker and contributor to entrepreneurial development and business growth & profitability radio shows (over 50 guest appearances). He also has his own blog as well as contributes to other blogs and business finance and management websites around the world. In addition to this book, Victor has also authored such books as "The Business You Can Start – Spotting the greatest opportunities in the economic downturn" - available on Amazon, Kindle (eBook edition), Barnes and Nobles, Vikebusinessservices.com and book stores near you on request. Victor's other upcoming books include, "Creating The Compelling Business Plan" and "Wealth creation as God intended."

21st Century Entrepreneurial Challenge Global Consortium - 21CECGC - is the brain child of Tonia and Victor with the vision to encourage and educate individuals, equipping them to make the right business decisions, and exposing them to opportunities of globalization towards a more secured and successful economic future. This publication along with other great resource tools are essential in making this vision a reality.

To request Victor and Tonia for speaking engagements, interviews and consultations please send an email to vito@21cecgc.com.

Address: 21CECGC 14241 Coursey Blvd, Suite A-12 #249, Baton Rouge, LA 70817.

21CECGC books are available at special discounts when purchased in bulk for promotions as well as for educational or fund raising activities.

Made in the USA
Charleston, SC
03 July 2013